Whose Gloves Are These?

A Look at Gloves Workers Wear—
Leather, Cloth, and Rubber

by Laura Purdie Salas

illustrated by Amy Bailey Muehlenhardt

PICTURE WINDOW BOOKS
Minneapolis, Minnesota

Special thanks to our advisers for their expertise:

Rick Levine, Publisher
Made To Measure and Uniform Market News Magazine
Highland Park, Illinois

Susan Kesselring, M.A., Literacy Educator
Rosemount–Apple Valley–Eagan (Minnesota) School District

Editor: Christianne Jones
Designer: Joe Anderson
Page Production: Amy Bailey Muehlenhardt
Editorial Director: Carol Jones
Creative Director: Keith Griffin
The illustrations in this book were created digitally.

Picture Window Books
5115 Excelsior Boulevard
Suite 232
Minneapolis, MN 55416
877-845-8392
www.picturewindowbooks.com

Printed in the United States of America.

Library of Congress Cataloging-in-Publication Data
Salas, Laura Purdie.
Whose gloves are these? : a look at gloves workers wear—leather, cloth, and rubber /
by Laura Purdie Salas ; illustrated by Amy Bailey Muehlenhardt.
p. cm. — (Whose is it?)
Includes bibliographical references and index.
ISBN 1-4048-1599-6 (hardcover)
1. Gloves—Juvenile literature. I. Muehlenhardt, Amy Bailey, 1974- ill. II. Title. III. Series.

GT2170.S25 2006
391.4'12—dc22   2005021848

Hold on tight and guess whose gloves are whose.

Sometimes workers wear gloves to protect their hands from injuries, germs, and harsh elements. Gloves can be thick or thin. They can be leather, rubber, or cloth. They can tell you about a worker's job.

Many people use their hands to do their work. Can you tell whose gloves are whose?

Look in the back for more information about gloves.

4

Whose glove is this,
so thick and long?

This is a zookeeper's glove.

Her gloves cover her hands and part of her arms. The gloves protect her from animals' sharp teeth and claws.

Fun Fact: When handling hedgehogs and porcupines, zookeepers wear heavy gloves to protect their hands and arms from the animals' quills.

Whose glove is this, so tough and oiled?

7

This is a baseball player's glove.

The ball comes flying toward him at 85 miles (136 kilometers) per hour. The glove protects the player's hand. He oils his glove to keep it soft.

Fun Fact: Baseball gloves are also called mitts.

8

Whose glove is this, so stretchy and thin?

9

This is a dentist's glove.

Her gloves are so thin she hardly feels them. These gloves protect the patient from the dentist's germs. They also protect the dentist from the patient's germs.

Fun Fact: Many doctors and dentists use gloves that have a light coating of powder inside them. The powder keeps their fingers from sticking to the glove.

Whose glove is this,
so bulky and warm?

11

This is a mountain guide's glove.

He helps people climb high in the mountains. The guide wears gloves to protect his hands from sharp rocks, insects, and plants. The gloves also keep his hands warm when the weather gets cold.

Fun Fact: Gloves are safety gear for guides. The frigid air on the top of mountains can freeze bare skin in 30 seconds.

Whose glove is this,
seeding and weeding?

This is a gardener's glove.

She wears her gloves while she takes care of plants, bushes, and trees. Her gloves protect her from thorny, scratchy plants like roses and raspberry bushes. They also keep her skin safe from poison ivy and dangerous chemicals.

Fun Fact: The gardener's gloves help her grip the tools so her hands don't rub on the tools' handles and give her blisters.

Whose gloves are these, so big and tough?

These are a welder's gloves.

A welder uses a small torch to connect
metal pieces by melting them together.
He helps build ships, cars, and bridges.
His gloves are fireproof and made of
heavy leather to protect him from
getting burned by his torch and
the hot metal.

Fun Fact: A welder's torch burns at more than 2,800 degrees Fahrenheit (1,538 degrees Celsius). That's hotter than the lava flowing out of a volcano!

Whose glove is this,
so rubbery and strong?

This is a housekeeper's glove.

She wears gloves while she cleans hotel rooms. She uses cleaners that could hurt her skin. She also gathers up trash. Her gloves keep her hands safe from chemicals and germs.

Fun Fact: A hotel housekeeper might clean 20 bedrooms and bathrooms every day.

Whose gloves are these,
knitted and striped?

These are your winter mittens!

They keep you warm while you roll in the snow. They keep your hands dry when you build a snowman. Do your parents remind you to wear your mittens every time you go outside in the cold?

Fun Fact: If you unraveled your mittens and stretched out the yarn, you might have 500 feet (153 meters) of yarn. If you could stretch that yarn up toward the sky, it would be as tall as a 50-story building.

Just for Fun

Whose glove is whose? Point to the picture
of the glove described in each sentence.

* My glove helps me catch flying balls.

baseball player's glove

* My gloves protect my hands from a hot flame.

welder's gloves

* My thin gloves protect me and my patients
from germs.

dentist's gloves

All About Gloves

Grooming Gloves

These gloves have rubber bristles or bumps on them. When you want to brush your cat or dog, you just pet them. The rubber bumps help remove the loose fur.

Gloves without Fingers

Some gloves have no fingers. They only cover the palms of your hands. People who lift weights use them so that barbells don't slip out of their hands.

Dusting Gloves

Sometimes cleaners and housekeepers wear dusting gloves. These very soft gloves won't scratch anything, and the fabric of the gloves traps the dirt in place.

Virtual Reality Gloves

People wear virtual gloves to explore a make-believe world on a computer. The glove has wires that tell the computer how you are moving your hand. When you move your hand, your make-believe hand on the computer screen moves the same way.

Glossary

barbell—a heavy bar with weights on the end of it

bristles—short, stiff hairs

fireproof—does not burn

injury—harm or damage done to a person or a thing

lava—soft, melted rock that flows out of a volcano

quills—sharp, needle-like coverings on an animal

unravel—to come undone

virtual reality—three-dimensional world created by a computer user where things on screen seem to come to life

To Learn More

At the Library

Adamson, Heather. *A Day in the Life of a Dentist*. Mankato, Minn.: Capstone Press, 2004.

LeBoutillier, Nate. *A Day in the Life of a Zookeeper*. Mankato, Minn.: Capstone Press, 2005.

Whitty, Helen. *Hats, Gloves, and Footwear*. Philadelphia: Chelsea House, 2001.

On the Web

FactHound offers a safe, fun way to find Internet sites related to this book. All of the sites on FactHound have been researched by our staff.

1. Visit *www.facthound.com*
2. Type in this special code for age-appropriate sites: 1404815996
3. Click on the FETCH IT button.

Your trusty FactHound will fetch the best sites for you!

Index

Look for all of the books in the Whose Is It? series:

Whose Coat Is This?
1-4048-1598-8

Whose Ears Are These?
1-4048-0004-2

Whose Eyes Are These?
1-4048-0005-0

Whose Feet Are These?
1-4048-0006-9

Whose Food Is This?
1-4048-0607-5

Whose Gloves Are These?
1-4048-1599-6

Whose Hat Is This?
1-4048-1600-3

Whose House Is This?
1-4048-0608-3

Whose Legs Are These?
1-4048-0007-7

Whose Mouth Is This?
1-4048-0008-5

Whose Nose Is This?
1-4048-0009-3

Whose Shadow Is This?
1-4048-0609-1

Whose Shoes Are These?
1-4048-1601-1

Whose Skin Is This?
1-4048-0010-7

Whose Sound Is This?
1-4048-0610-5

Whose Spots Are These?
1-4048-0611-3

Whose Tail Is This?
1-4048-0011-5

Whose Tools Are These?
1-4048-1602-X

Whose Vehicle Is This?
1-4048-1603-8

Whose Work Is This?
1-4048-0612-1